W9-BEN-232

Watch a flea jump in slow motion!

Meet a supersized tardigrade!

Make a nasty tick crawl along your hand!

Explore the app to discover incredible facts and stats about the micro monsters!

Published in 2017 by Carlton Books Limited
An imprint of the Carlton Publishing Group
20 Mortimer Street, London W1T 3JW

A catalogue record for this book is available from the British Library.

ISBN: 978-1-78312-256-1
Printed in Dongguan, China

Executive editors: Anna Brett, Jo Casey
Design & illustrations: WildPixel Ltd.
Cover illustration: WildPixel Ltd.
Picture research: Steve Behan
Digital producer: Sean Daly
Production: Yael Steinitz

Need some help? Check out our useful website
for helpful tips and problem-solving advice:

www.icarlton.co.uk/help

iEXPLORE

MICRO MONSTERS

Camilla de la Bédoyère

CARLTON KIDS

A HIDDEN WORLD

Welcome to the micro world of living things, where tiny terrors and mini-monsters roam! You might not have realised this part of the animal kingdom existed, but thanks to the brilliance of scientists, engineers and photographers we can now reveal all types of microlife, and discover their amazing secrets. Before the invention of microscopes and magnifying lenses, this mysterious world was hidden from view – but now we can enjoy it in all its gruesome, incredible glory.

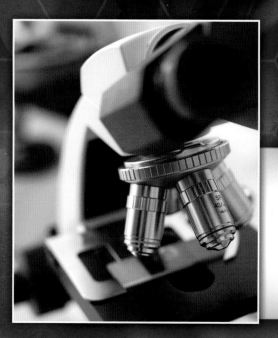

WHAT IS A MICROSCOPE?

A microscope is a piece of equipment that allows us to see very small things that our eyes are not good enough to see. It magnifies things (makes them look larger), usually with the help of a lens.

THE SIZE OF LIVING THINGS

We measure large animals in metres (m) and centimetres (cm): a blue whale, for example, measures up to 30 m long. Small things are measured in millimetres (mm) (there are 10 mm in 1 cm) and even smaller units. Microscopic things are smaller than 0.1 mm long and we can only see them with the help of a microscope. An ordinary microscope can magnify an object about 1,000 times, but an electron microscope can magnify objects or parts of a living thing more than one million times!

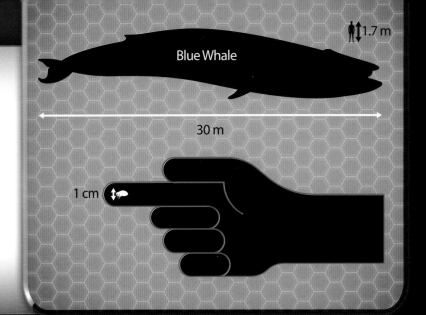

↕ 1.7 m

Blue Whale

30 m

1 cm

A magnified silkworm larva.

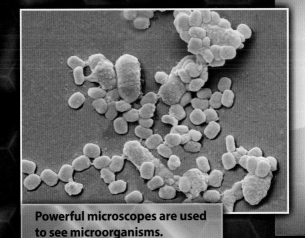

Powerful microscopes are used to see microorganisms.

DISCOVERING MICROLIFE

The first person to see microorganisms was a Dutch scientist called Antony van Leeuwenhoek, in the 17th century. Around the same time, an English scientist called Robert Hooke built a light microscope that enabled him to magnify objects up to 500 times. As technology improved, microscopes produced bigger, better images and in the 1930s the first electron microscope was invented.

MICRO FACT

Scientist van Leeuwenhoek called microorganisms 'animalcules' or 'tiny animals'.

MICROLIFE IN OUR WORLD

Microorganisms are essential to human health, and the survival of all other forms of life on Earth. They help create the gases we breathe, allow us to digest our food and provide food for other animals. They also live on dead animals and plants and break them down into useful substances that allows new life to begin. However, microorganisms can cause harm by spreading disease and producing gases and other chemicals that pollute our environment.

FLEA

There are about 2,400 species of flea, and all of them are bloodsucking parasites. Most are harmless to people, although they are often an irritating pest for our pets. The Oriental rat flea, however, has a bad reputation because it carries the plague – a disease that can kill humans.

Fleas jump or crawl but cannot fly.

MAGNIFICATION: x 50

A flea uses its long spring-like hind legs to leap.

A SPRING IN THEIR STEP

Fleas are amongst the most impressive jumpers in the animal kingdom. Many types can keep leaping for hours without getting tired, and a cat flea can travel 34 cm in a single jump. That's the equivalent of a human jumping 70 times their own body length – further than a football pitch! They can achieve this incredible feat thanks to a pad of rubber-like material in their legs, which releases enough energy for them to accelerate at high speed.

MICRO FACT

In the 14th century an estimated 25 million died from the Black Plague carried by the Oriental rat flea.

SNEAKY AND SPEEDY

The animal or plant that a parasite lives on is called a 'host'. Fleas scurry about between the strands of hair, feathers or fur on their host. They have piercing mouthparts for inserting into flesh and sucking up blood. After a blood meal females can begin to lay their eggs. Worm-like larvae hatch from the eggs and fall to the ground, the floor, or the host animal's bed where they live on dried blood or adult flea faeces until they are ready to grow.

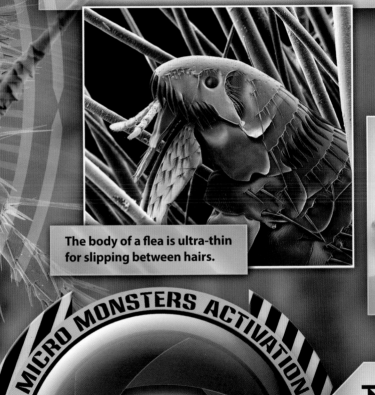

The body of a flea is ultra-thin for slipping between hairs.

SILKEN COCOONS

When the larvae are ready to turn into adults they spin silken cocoons around themselves and begin to transform into jumping blood-suckers. When they emerge from their cocoons the fleas are fully-equipped with their super springy legs. They can detect the body heat of a host animal – or the carbon dioxide it breathes out – and leap up into its fur, ready to start the life cycle all over again.

A cocooned larva can turn into an adult in less than five days.

MICRO MONSTERS ACTIVATION

Watch the incredible jump of the flea in slow motion.

THE DEADLIEST FLEA

Most fleas are just a nuisance, but the Oriental rat flea is deadly. It's host to a bacterium called Yersinia pestis which causes a terrible human disease: plague. The fleas that carry plague are unable to feed properly, so they vomit blood and bacteria back into their hosts and immediately go in search of a new host. This causes the plague to pass quickly through a population, wiping out thousands of lives at a time. Thankfully, plague is now very rare and can be treated with antibiotics.

A rat flea can live for more than a year in the right conditions.

EYELASH MITE

Do you want to know something to make your skin crawl? Your face is home to microscopic beasties that come to life and scamper about at night when you are asleep! Eyelash mites feast on your skin cells and the oily secretions that keep your skin supple and smooth. The good news is they generally don't do any harm!

HAPPY FAMILIES

Male and female mites meet up around the rim of a hair follicle at mating time. Females lay their eggs deep inside the follicle or a sebaceous gland (which makes sebum). Tiny baby mites hatch from the eggs after just two days. As they mature, they crawl over the skin to find their own pores to settle down in to. Mites don't like bright lights, so this is why they are most active at night when you're asleep. They live for just two weeks.

GOOD OR BAD?

These creepy critters have lived on humans for millions of years and potentially go unnoticed for your entire life. However, eyelash mite populations can grow out of control, causing sore skin and swollen eyelids. Some people are also allergic to the mites, or they possibly react to the bacteria that live inside the mites' bodies.

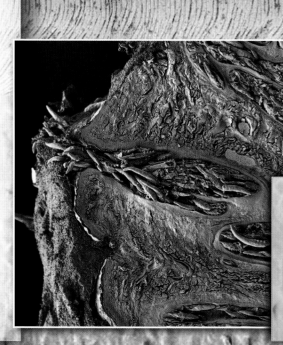

One hair follicle may be home to many mites!

A SNUG HOME

The eyelash mite's long, slender body is the perfect shape for burrowing into skin pores. These tiny holes in human skin are where your hair grows. As the root grows it is bathed in oily sebum, which mites love. So the mite lies head-down in the pore and uses its clawed mouthparts to grip onto the cells that produce this oil, so it can suck out the contents. Not all pores on your body are home to a mite – they much prefer places where there is plenty of sebum, such as your eyelids, nose, cheeks and chin.

The mites (in blue) lie head-down next to a strand of hair (in yellow).

Bacteria thrive where mites damage a dog's skin, and cause mange.

MIGHTY DOG MITES

Although there are only two species of mites that live on humans, there are plenty of others that live on animals. Demodex canis, for example, lives on dogs' skin. A puppy gets its mites from its mother, when feeding on her milk or snuggling up close to her. Some dogs react very badly to their mites, and suffer a painful skin condition called mange.

MICRO FACT

These mites never poop. They store all their waste in their bodies and when they die a lifetime's worth of poop is released… on to your face!

An eyelash mite has eight fat little legs for crawling.

MICRO MONSTERS ACTIVATION

Inspect an eyelash mite in all its gory detail.

TARDIGRADE

Meet the invincible, indestructible, truly incredible tardigrade! This minibeast has mind-blowing superpowers and its family has survived on the planet for hundreds of millions of years. Scientists are only just beginning to learn about this animal, even though billions of them live alongside us. Tiny tardigrades are also known as 'moss piglets' or 'water bears'.

MAGNIFICATION: X 330

SURVIVORS

Moss piglets have been sent into space to find out if they could survive with no air, gravity, food or water. The minibeasts were attached to a satellite to fly through space before returning home. Many of them survived and some even laid eggs that hatched! This is an amazing feat because the tardigrades were exposed to cosmic radiation and other hazards that would leave any other animal dead!

Tardigrades have eight legs in total, each with tiny claws.

MICRO FACT

Tardigrades are called micro-animals because they are some of the smallest animals ever discovered – they are almost impossible to see without a microscope.

ANCIENT ANIMALS

Tardigrades have been around for at least 500 million years. That makes them some of the oldest animals on Earth. Their ancient history has made it difficult for scientists to work out exactly what type of animals they are – or even what animals they are related to!

Tardigrades were first discovered in 1773 by a German zoologist.

Tardigrades can survive in temperatures as low as -272°C.

SIMPLE LIVES

There are about 1,000 different species of tardigrade, and most of them live on plants such as moss, algae and lichens. They use their eight clawed-legs to slowly creep between the plants, sucking up their juices. (The name 'tardigrade' means slow-stepper.)

A tardigrade tun can exist like this for up to ten years!

SUPER POWERS

A tardigrade can survive being frozen, boiled, crushed, left to dry out and even put in the vacuum of space. These super powers explain why moss piglets can be found on mountaintops, in the freezing Antarctic, under the deep ocean – and in more obvious places such as gardens and rooftops. They can survive some extreme situations by hibernating, drying out their bodies and protecting their DNA from damage. When they are in this desiccated state they are called 'tuns'. If a tun gets wet it can spring back to life, even after many years.

MICRO MONSTERS ACTIVATION

Meet a supersized tardigrade and make it creep around your room!

TICK

With their plump little bodies and four pairs of legs, these tiny terrors may look creepy, but not particularly dangerous. Don't be fooled! Ticks are blood-sucking parasites with a deadly secret. Their spit can harbour a whole range of nasty microorganisms that spread disease to animals and humans.

An adult deer tick.

The rash caused by Lyme disease.

DEADLY DISEASES

When ticks suck on their host's blood they can pass over various forms of microlife in their saliva. These include bacteria, viruses and protozoa (tiny single-celled organisms), which can harm the host. Lyme disease affects humans who have been bitten by deer ticks that are infected with a type of bacteria called a spirochaete. It causes pain in the joints, and can leave people unwell for many years. It's also very difficult to treat.

WHAT IS A PARASITE?

Parasites are animals or plants that live on, or in, another living thing (their host) and cause it harm. Parasites feed on their host but they can also spread diseases to it. The disease does far more harm to the host than to the parasite, but generally a parasite doesn't want to kill its host and leave itself homeless and hungry!

MICRO FACT

A tick can live for up to three years, but many die young because they starve to death before finding a host.

FAST FACTS

TYPE: Arachnid
FOUND: Worldwide
HABITAT: On animals and land
DIET: Blood

Up to 1 cm long

SUCKING BLOOD

A tick nestles in between strands of the host's hair and grabs hold of its skin, cutting into it. It forces its feeding tube into the flesh and starts to suck blood. As it sucks, a tick may pass a special pain-relieving spit into the host so the host doesn't notice it is under attack. Some types of tick have toxic spit that may kill small, weak animal hosts up to a week later. As the tick feeds, its body swells up. Once it's full of blood, the tick lets go of the skin and falls off the host.

TICK LIFE CYCLE

1.
2.
3.
4.

1. Eggs
2. Larva
3. Nymph
4. Adult

BIZARRE LIVES

Most ticks have four stages in their life cycle: egg; larva with six legs; nymph with eight legs; and adult. Once a tick has hatched from its egg it relies on meals of blood to survive throughout its life. Larvae and nymphs are usually parasites on different animals to their adults. Deer tick larvae and nymphs, for example, feed on rats, birds and mice rather than deer.

HUNTING FOR HOSTS

When they are not feeding, ticks live on or near plants, often by the side of paths that host animals regularly use. They use their hind-legs to cling to leaves and reach out with their front legs and wait until an animal passes by. Then they jump aboard and grab onto the animal's hair. Ticks sense an animal is close by detecting breath, body smells, heat, movement and even shadows.

MICRO MONSTERS ACTIVATION

Make this nasty tick crawl along your hand as it hunts for blood.

BED BUGS

Home is where the heart is... but it's also where millions of micro-beasts roam, munching their way through the debris, dust and detritus of human life. And nowhere is free from their attention, not even a clean bed or a well-vacuumed carpet, which is where bed bugs like to live.

NIGHTMARE BUGS

A hundred years ago many homes were shared with bed bugs – nasty blood-sucking insects that feed on sleeping people. Their numbers fell when people's homes became less crowded and cleaner, but they have become more common again in recent years.

Sucking mouthparts (centre) are called 'stylets'.

MICRO FACT

Bed bugs can survive for many months without eating if necessary.

MAGNIFICATION: X 10

BLOOD-SUCKERS

Bed bugs belong to a group of insects called 'true bugs', which have long, slender sucking mouthparts. They use these mouthparts to pierce human skin and drink blood. As they feed, they inject chemicals that stop the blood from clotting and make the area of skin around the wound go numb. This means the victim is unaware they are being fed on. Later, these bite-wounds can become very sore and itchy. Beds are perfect places for these bugs because they are warm and moist – and often contain humans!

These sores are a sign that bed bugs have been feasting on this person!

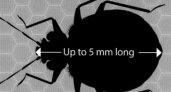

← Up to 5 mm long →

TYPE: Insect
FOUND: Worldwide
HABITAT: In human dwellings
DIET: Blood

The hard skin of a bug is flat and tough to protect it from damage.

Dust mites have eight legs and are arachnids, like spiders and scorpions.

DUST MITE INVASION

Dust mites live alongside bed bugs at home as they love to feed on dust. There can be as many as 5,000 mites feeding on a single gram of dust! Dead human skin cells form a major part of the 'dust' you'll find at home, and they create a perfect supply of food for dust mites.

MICRO MONSTERS ACTIVATION

Watch out for nasty bed bug bites as the tiny terrors crawl on your skin!

PREVENTION OR CURE?

Dust mites may be useful in cleaning up after us, but unfortunately they also create their own mess, pooping almost as fast as they eat! Their waste can cause allergic reactions in people and pets. It's impossible to remove dust mites completely, although a clean, cool and dry home, with plenty of fresh air, is less welcoming to these little beasts and their friends the bed bugs.

APHID

Look closely at the tender stems of a plant in spring, and you may spy a cluster of soft, green bodies. These little bugs are feasting on the juices inside the plant. It's easy to overlook aphids, but don't be fooled by their simple appearance. These micro monsters have a few surprises in store!

An aphid's colour often matches the colour of its host plant.

GREENFLY

Aphids are true bugs and are also known as greenflies – although they can be other colours including black, pink or yellow. They are bugs with six legs and soft, squashy bodies and antennae. Some aphids also have wings. Aphids feed by using their sucking mouthparts to pierce plants and drink their sap. They are often found near the soft and tender parts of plants, such as flower buds and leaf buds. Removing sap damages plants, but aphids can cause even greater damage by spreading diseases between species.

MAGNIFICATION: X 45

SECRET WEAPON

As aphids feed on a plant's sweet sap a huge amount of sugar enters their bodies. To avoid exploding in a sticky mess, they pass a gooey substance out of their abdomen to get rid of the excess. It's called honeydew because it is sugary, but it also contains chemicals that further damage a plant.

Honeydew is released from two tubes called 'cornicles'.

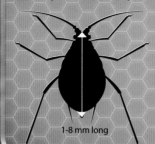

1-8 mm long

TYPE: Insect
FOUND: Worldwide
HABITAT: On plants
DIET: Plant sap

Most aphids are wingless and stay on one plant all their lives.

Ladybird beetles and their larvae eat aphids.

PESTS WITH A PLACE

Aphids may be pests, but they have an important place in nature. Ants feed on the honeydew that aphids make, so they try to protect the aphids from other predators to guarantee they have a ready supply of honeydew. Unfortunately, many are still doomed to die in the mouths of other animals as they are an essential food source for insects, spiders, birds and frogs.

MICRO MONSTERS ACTIVATION

Watch incredible aphids crawl around your room!

SUPER FEMALES

Female aphids can reproduce without mating! This incredible skill is called parthenogenesis. The first eggs that hatch in spring are all females and they make clones (identical copies of themselves). This way of reproducing is fast and simple because the females don't have to find mates – and a population of aphids can rapidly explode in number. These females don't lay eggs: they keep the eggs inside themselves and give birth to nymphs, which rapidly grow into adults.

ANTARCTIC KRILL

Far away, in the Southern Ocean, billions of shrimp-like animals called krill swarm in the icy waters of the Antarctic. They attract animals from all over the world to this bleak and windswept location as they are an important food source. Krill may be small, but they make an enormous impact on the lives of our planet's marine mammals and fish.

MICRO FACT

If an Antarctic krill can escape the jaws of a whale or other predators it can live for up to seven years!

LITTLE PREY, BIG PREDATORS

Krill's shrimp-like bodies are made up of many segments, with legs on either side. They feed on microscopic animals and plants in the water. A single krill wouldn't make much of a meal for a large marine mammal. However, as millions of krill exist in the ocean, they are a perfect source of nutrition for many animals including fish, penguins, seals and seabirds. In fact, many animals migrate specially to the Southern Ocean to feed on them. Just one cubic metre of seawater can hold 30,000 krill.

Adelie penguins feed krill to their chicks who are too young to swim.

MAGNIFICATION: x5

SAFETY IN NUMBERS

A swarm, or group, of krill is called a school. The krill swim closely together as a school because this offers them some defence from the fish that gather around them, trying to grab a bite. The krill swirl and spin in a huge pink cloud, making it harder for fish to find a single krill to catch. Of course there's nothing they can do against a blue whale, which eats up to 4 tonnes of krill a day!

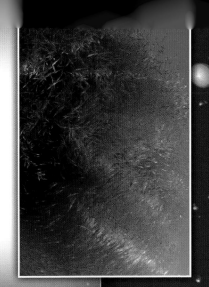

ON THE MOVE

Winter in the Southern Ocean is long and extremely cold. Many animals, including krill, struggle to survive the near-freezing temperatures, so they disappear to the sea's depths. Here the water is less affected by the wintry weather. Krill also make shorter journeys every day in the summer, as they move up and down in the water. During the night they stay near the surface to feed, but in the daytime they sink below 20 metres to avoid predators. This daily movement is called a vertical migration (because it's up and down!).

MICRO MONSTERS ACTIVATION

See amazing Antarctic krill up close!

A fishing boat, or trawler, gathers krill from depths of up to 250 metres.

THE FUTURE OF KRILL

Scientists have no idea how many krill live in the sea, and their estimates vary from 125 to 750 million metric tons! However, they do believe that the numbers of krill have fallen dramatically in recent years. Huge trawlers collect krill to sell as food for humans and animals, and because krill is a valuable source of protein, fishing for krill will probably increase. Sadly, this could damage the populations of whales and other marine animals that rely on krill for food.

HEAD LOUSE

Head lice are close to being the perfect human parasites. They have lived with us (and on us) for millions of years, and despite the best efforts of scientists and doctors, they have survived endless onslaughts with chemical shampoos and nit combs! Lice may be irritating, but their unique lifestyle is also impressive.

Unlike many parasites, lice spend their whole lives on a host.

SUITED TO SCALPS

Head lice have only one habitat: the human head. Their little bodies are perfectly adapted for a life spent disappearing between strands of hair, making it difficult to see, catch or remove them. A louse has a pale, soft, flat body and short, clawed legs that can grip on to strands of hair. They are not great movers because they can't jump, fly, swim or burrow, but they do nestle into the dark, warm parts of a head, and scuttle away from light. The nape of the neck and the warm areas behind ears are their favourite spots!

MICRO FACT

In one of the worst cases of head lice ever recorded, a child had more than 2,600 of the blood-sucking creatures on their head!

MAGNIFICATION: X 10

FEELING LOUSY?

Although lice feed on human blood several times a day, the amount they devour is so tiny that the blood loss doesn't harm their host. However, their bites, their saliva and their faeces can make the host's skin very itchy. Lice are common in schoolchildren, and having clean hair doesn't prevent an infection. Lice will climb aboard anyone's hair if they get the chance! It takes less than 30 seconds for a louse to clamber from one head to another.

You can't feel the bite, but it can make your skin itchy afterwards.

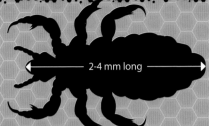

2-4 mm long

TYPE: Insect
FOUND: Worldwide
HABITAT: On human scalps
DIET: Blood

If left untreated, lice can make thousands of eggs.

This unhatched egg case has been magnified 145 times. It is cemented to a strand of hair.

EGGS AND NITS

A female louse can live for 6–7 weeks on a head, and can lay more than 100 eggs in that time. Each yellow egg is glued to a strand of hair, usually close to the warm scalp. When a nymph hatches, its empty egg case turns white, and is known as a 'nit'. The glue that binds a nit to the hair is so strong it may stick for weeks or even months! The nymph grows and moults three times before it becomes an adult. A female begins laying eggs about seven days later.

MICRO MONSTERS ACTIVATION

Guide the gruesome head louse up and down a strand of hair!

SMALL SURVIVORS

Head lice have breathing holes in their skin. They can avoid drowning when a person washes their head by closing these holes, and holding their breath! Lice have become resistant to many pesticide shampoos that have been used to get rid of them, which explains why millions of people still suffer from head lice infestations every year, all over the world.

The fine teeth of a nit comb dislodge lice and their eggs.

VIRUSES AND BACTERIA

The most important members of the micro monster community are bacteria and viruses. These microscopic life-forms are found everywhere on Earth! They are far too small to be seen with the naked eye, and not even a regular microscope is powerful enough to zoom in on a tiny virus.

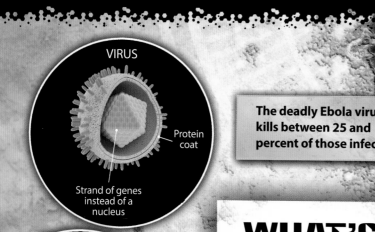

VIRUS

Protein coat

Strand of genes instead of a nucleus

The deadly Ebola virus kills between 25 and 90 percent of those infected.

BACTERIA

Cell wall

Cell membrane

Cytoplasm

Chromosome instead of a nucleus

Flagellum

WHAT'S THE DIFFERENCE?

A single bacterium is one cell with DNA inside and a cell wall. Some types also have tails called flagella that allow them to swim. A virus is just a simple unit made up of DNA coated in a layer of protein – it's not a full cell. Bacteria are bigger than viruses and can reproduce themselves, whereas viruses have to attach themselves to other cells in order to multiply.

MAGNIFICATION: X 12,000

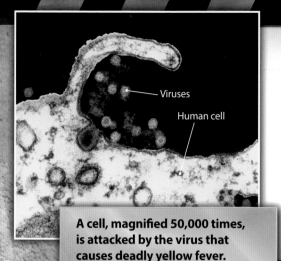

Viruses

Human cell

A cell, magnified 50,000 times, is attacked by the virus that causes deadly yellow fever.

PATHOGENS

Although many bacteria are harmless, or even essential to life on Earth, others spread disease like viruses. These are called pathogens. Viral pathogens cause measles, yellow fever, flu, rubella and even the common cold. Bacterial pathogens cause skin infections, food poisoning and tooth decay, as well as deadly diseases such as typhus and plague (see pages 8–9).

(see pages 8–9)

FAST FACTS

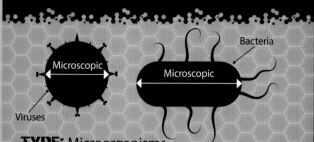

Bacteria

Microscopic

Microscopic

Viruses

TYPE: Microorganisms
FOUND: Worldwide
HABITAT: Everywhere
DIET: Viruses do not eat. Bacteria eat what they live on, or make food by photosynthesis.

Scientists use powerful electron microscopes to see viruses and bacteria.

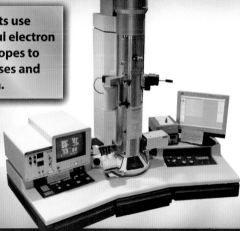

MICRO FACT

In 1918–19 a deadly type of flu virus spread rapidly around the world, killing more than 20 million people.

VIRAL ATTACK

A virus is a strange type of life-form that challenges our idea of what a 'living thing' actually is. It cannot exist on its own, so it must hijack another organism, invading its cells and forcing them to make copies of the virus. Eventually, the cells die but the virus spreads and infects other healthy cells. Viruses are the smallest living things yet discovered, and they are so small that scientists can only study them using electron microscopes.

GOOD BACTERIA

Without bacteria there would be no humans, or even life on Earth as we know it! This is because bacteria produce oxygen – the gas that humans and other animals need to breathe. Bacteria were some of the first living things on planet Earth and around three billion years ago they had released enough oxygen into the atmosphere for more complex types of life to start to appear. They do other important jobs too: bacteria in the human gut help to break down our food so we can use it for energy. They also help decompose animal bodies and dead plants, and are used to make cheese and medicines.

Bacteria (green) in the stomach can be harmless, but in large numbers they can damage the stomach's lining (purple).

RAGWORM

This brutal beastie may look like an alien, but it's actually a native of Planet Earth! Ragworms live in soft sand under the sea where they pursue their prey of small crustaceans and molluscs. Ragworms are good at hiding, so it's a rare treat to see one up close in all of its fascinating detail!

A ragworm is at home in the soft sand in shallow seawater.

ON THE HUNT

Ragworms are good swimmers, but they prefer to spend their time hiding in U-shaped burrows, which they dig in soft sand and mud. Here they lie in wait, leaping out to grab prey in their mouths when it passes by. If they are short of food, ragworms will eat the top layer of mud and sand, extracting tiny morsels of food from it. They will also scavenge the remains of dead animals. But to catch their favourite food of shrimps and small crabs, they will happily chase through the open water.

MICRO FACT

King ragworms live in the Atlantic Ocean and have been known to grow to more than 120 cm long!

NASTY NIPPERS

Ragworms' pincer-like mouthparts have super-strong teeth made from metal zinc, rather than calcium, like human teeth. They crush the ragworm's prey and will deliver a nasty bite to a human finger or toe! A ragworm's mouth connects directly to its gut, which runs down the length of the body and ends with the anus, in the worm's tail.

Four white, sharp teeth grow around the worm's mouth.

SEGMENTED WORMS

Ragworms belong to an enormous family of worms called annelids. An annelid's body is long and slender, and divided into segments. Ragworms can have up to 200 segments in their body, most of which have bristly legs that are used to move the ragworm quickly towards its prey.

TIME TO CHANGE

Ragworms can only mate and breed once before they die. They may be able to mate after just one year, but the larger types generally need to be two or three years old. Their bodies begin to change in preparation for breeding – their eyes grow larger and they gain swimming legs so they can seek out a mate more easily.

A young ragworm floats in the sea and is called a larva.

MICRO MONSTERS ACTIVATION

Meet a giant ragworm!

PSEUDOSCORPION

If you shared your home with one of these menacing mini-monsters you'd like to know, wouldn't you? Well, you probably do – but don't worry because, despite their fearsome appearance, pseudoscorpions are harmless to humans. Small insects, however, do have good reason to fear those venomous pincers!

FALSE SCORPIONS

Pseudoscorpions belong to the class of eight-legged invertebrates called arachnids, along with spiders, ticks, mites and scorpions. The prefix 'pseudo' means false, so these animals are also known as false scorpions. They may look similar, but pseudoscorpions don't have a stinging tail like scorpions. This predator's body is pear-shaped, with a plump abdomen and no tail. Colours vary from pale brown to black, sometimes with a hint of red or orange.

MAGNIFICATION: X 200

When magnified, the tooth-like edges of a pseudoscorpion's pincers are visible.

SCISSOR-HANDS

The huge, scary-looking pincers at the arachnid's front end are called pedipalps and they are essential weapons in this mini-predator's quest for food. Pedipalps have a claw, with 'fingers' and a venom gland. When a pseudoscorpion spies a victim, it hunts it and grabs it with its pedipalps, gripping and crushing it whilst also forcing venom into it. The venom disables the prey, which means it can be passed into the pseudoscorpion's mouth where it is crunched by tough mouthparts.

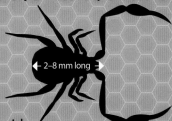
MICRO FACT

At mating time, male pseudoscorpions perform a special dance to impress the females!

A group of hungry hunters gather to eat a fly.

SECRETIVE HUNTERS

Pseudoscorpions eat small insects and mites. Because they hunt pests, such as clothes moth larvae, they are generally welcome in human homes, although they are so small and secretive they are rarely seen. Pseudoscorpions live in dark places, so their eyesight is not good. Some species have two eyes, some have four, and some are completely blind!

MICRO MONSTERS ACTIVATION

Watch out for the pseudoscorpion's scary pincers!

GOOD MOTHERS

Female pseudoscorpions carry their eggs on their abdomen while they develop, and the babies stay with their mother for a short time after hatching. As they grow they moult their skin. Some species will even spin a silken tent around themselves for protection when doing this.

MICRO FACTS

Microorganisms that can live in harsh environments are called extremophiles, which means 'lovers of the extreme'.

A dust mite is so small it could easily perch on the point of a sewing needle.

Bacteria on teeth feed on sugars and make acids that damage tooth enamel, causing decay.

There are up to a million microbes living on just a square centimetre of skin. Most of them are harmless, or helpful.

Rainforest sloths grow green fur because microscopic algae (simple green plants) live in their strands of hair!

Some ticks are so tough they can withstand being stood on, but if they have just fed they are likely to explode, sending blood flying in all directions!

Tiny booklice are just 2 mm long. They destroy books by eating the glue that holds the pages together.

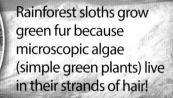

Before the days of modern science and microscopes, people believed that rotting meat turned into maggots!